T0068230

THE PRAYERS
OF THE
RIGHTEOUS KEYS
AND **TOOLS** TO AN
EFFECTIVE
PRAYER LIFE

PROPHETESS LEONIE WALTERS

WESTBOW
PRESS°
A DIVISION OF THOMAS NELSON
& ZONDERVAN

WestBow Press books may be ordered through booksellers or by contacting:

WestBow Press
A Division of Thomas Nelson & Zondervan
1663 Liberty Drive
Bloomington, IN 47403
www.westbowpress.com
844-714-3454

ISBN: 978-1-6642-5605-7 (sc)
ISBN: 978-1-6642-5604-0 (e)

Print information available on the last page.

WestBow Press rev. date: 2/7/2022

Contents

Contents

I Greet you in the mighty name of Jesus Christ our Lord and savior. I pray that as you read this book you will be inspired and motivated to spend more time in prayer and draw closer to the Lord if you have not been doing so, sacrifice some time to pray out of your busy schedules and as you pray the instructions that the Lord gives you through dreams, vision, or audible voice you will act upon his instructions promptly, why? because some instructions that the Lord gives to us we must move in the proper timing, if we delay or move before the time it can be catastrophic, we can miss our season, as well as the people around us may be in danger, because 1Peter 5:8 NKJV says; Be sober, be vigilant; because your adversary the devil walks about like a roaring lion, seeking whom he may devour and so God sometimes allow you to stand in the gap for the people around you, your family members, for your church sisters and brothers in Christ Jesus, for your community, for your leaders and for those who are in Authority over us 1Timothy 2:2]. Prayer should not just be for some of us our first response when we are face with difficult issues in our lives, but prayer should be an essential part of our day-to-day routine or one of our day-to day accomplishment. When we abide in the presence of the Lord, we will become more and more sensitive to the Holy spirit, and we will also grow tremendously spiritually. Being in the presence of the Lord consistently and earnestly will bring about changes in our lives for example the way we see things and do things will be different than before [our day-to-day operation will be different] because his ways are not our ways, neither are his thought our thought. Jeremiah 10:23 [NKJV] Jeremiah said, O Lord, I know the way of man is not in himself; it is not in man who walks to direct his own steps. It is in prayer that we get directions, instructions and are strengthened in the inner man. Jude 1: 20 NIV says; But you, dear friends, by building yourselves up in your most holy faith and praying in the Holy Spirit. When we pray in the Holy spirit, we are building up ourselves spiritually. The name of Jesus is a strong tower Philippians 2:9-10 NIV Says; Therefore, God exalted him to the highest place and gave him the name that is above every name, that at the name of Jesus every knee should bow, in heaven and on earth and under the earth and every tongue acknowledge that Jesus Christ is Lord, to the glory of God the father. There is power in the name of Jesus, power to heal, power to deliver, power to break chains and bondage, power to bring you out of any kind of situations, power to transform, power to overthrow the plots, schemes, and devices of the enemy. The name of Jesus is a strong tower the righteous run into it, and they are saved.

The heavens declare the glory of God; and the firmament sheweth his handywork (Psalm 19:1 KJV)

John 15:7 (amp) If you remain in me and my words remain in you [that is, if we are vitally united and my message lives in your heart], ask whatever you wish and it will be done for you.

If we abide in God and his word abide in us, we can ask anything in Jesus name and it will be done. The key word is abide or remain in him and his word abide or remain in us. We abide in him by staying in his presence consistently, studying and meditate upon his word so that it takes root and remain in us that we can remain in him. John 1:1 NIV; says the word was with God and the word was God. The word of God is a powerful tool to an effective prayer life and to remain and abide in him. We must take up a permanent resident in him to remain stable in him. 2 Timothy 2:11-13 amp says, if we died with him, we will also live with him; if we endure, we will also reign with him; If we deny him, he will also deny us; If we are faithless, he remains faithful [true to his word and his righteous character], for he cannot deny himself.

[1] To be stable in God it starts with a stable mind our mindset must change

To have a stable mind we need to be renewed in our minds and transformation brings about a renewed mind._when we are transformed our mind will be renewed. Submitting to the word of God brings about transformation by Allowing the word of God to wash us, cleanse us, corrects us and mold us, it illuminates us and brings about a transformation in and around us. [These are some scriptures that you can read. 2 Corinthians 5:17 amp says, Therefore if anyone is in Christ [that is, grafted in, joined to him by faith in him as Savior], he is a new creature [reborn and renewed by the Holy Spirit]; the old things [the previous moral and spiritual condition] have passed away. Behold, new things have come [because spiritual awakening brings a new life]. Philippians 2:5, Matthew 22:37. Colossians 3:2 NIV says, Set your minds on things above, not on earthly things. [Romans 12:3 NIV] says and I quote, we should not think more highly of ourselves than we ought to but be sober in our Judgement according to the faith that God has given unto us. [You can read James1:5-8 KJV a double-minded man is unstable in all is ways. It takes a made-up mindset with the help of the Holy Spirit to truly serve God in spirit and in truth, you must want it. It's an act of your will, when you are undecided that's not a good place to be. When you are trying to achieve something, you will make- up your mind first that no matter what you face you are going to get where you need to go it starts in your mind. Romans 12:2 amp says; And do not be conformed to this world [any longer with its superficial values and customs], but be transformed and progressively changed [as you mature spiritually] by the renewing of your mind [focusing on godly values and ethical attitudes], so that you may prove [for yourselves] what the will of God is, that which is good and acceptable and perfect [in his plan and purpose for you].

[2] To be stable in God, we must walk in obedience to his word [he is the word]. [John 14:15]. Matthew 7:24-25 NIV says; "Therefore everyone who hears these words of mine and puts them into practice is like a wise man who build his house on the rock. The rain came down, the streams rose,

and the winds blew and beat against that house; yet it did not fall, because it had its foundation on the rock. Your Obedience to God carry prosperity, a long life, and a solid foundation. God is just asking for us to love, trust him and obey his commandments [read Deuteronomy 6,7] John 15:14 amp says; You are my friends if you keep on doing what I command you.

[3] To be stable in God, we must live a righteous and holy life before him. These are some scriptures that you can meditate upon 1Peter 1: 15-16, Leviticus 19:2, Romans 12:1, Titus 2:14, Matthew 6:33, Matthew 5:10, Psalms 34:19, Proverbs 11:30,1John 2:29, Psalms 37: 25, Proverbs 4:18, Proverbs 12:3(amp) A man will not be established by wickedness, But the root of the [consistently] righteous will not be moved. Titus 2: 11-12AMP] For the [remarkable, undeserved] grace of God that brings salvation has appeared to all men. It teaches us to reject ungodliness and worldly (immoral) desires, and to live sensible, upright, and godly lives [lives with a purpose that reflect spiritual maturity] in this present age. James 1:21amp says. So get rid of all uncleanness and all that remains of wickedness, and with a humble spirit receive the word [of God] which is implanted [actually rooted in your heart], which is able to save your souls.

[4] To be stable in God we must walk in love because God is love. [love one another] these are some scriptures that you can meditate upon 1 Corinthians 13:1-13, John 13:34, 1John 4:20, 1Peter 4:8, John 13:34-35, Romans 12:10, 1John 4:7-10, Romans 13:8] 1John 3:18 NIV; Dear children, let us not love with words or speech but with actions and in truth. Love is an action word. where are our deeds behind our love for one another, when you love someone, you show them that you love them, you will put your love on display by sending them flowers, buying them gifts, and showing them affection, you genuinely care for that person and sometimes a person will do all of that but have an agender because their hearts are not in the right place, but am taking about genuine love the agape love. the word of God says for God so love the world that he gave

his only begotten son John 3:16 KJV. Our heavenly Father exhibit his love for us all and he is a perfect example of love because he is love. 1 Corinthians 13:4-7 NKJV] Love suffers long and is kind; love does not envy; love does not parade itself, is not puffed up; does not behave rudely, does not seek its own, is not provoked, thinks no evil; does not rejoice in iniquity, but rejoices in the truth; bears all things, believes all things, hopes all things, endures all things. Love must be sincere.

[5] To be stable in God we must walk in Humility, and these are some scriptures you can meditate upon. 1 Peter 5: 6-7, Colossians 3:12 NIV Therefore, as God's chosen people, holy and dearly loved, clothe yourselves with compassion, kindness, humility, gentleness, and patience. Proverbs 11:2 NIV says; When pride comes, then comes disgrace, but with humility comes wisdom. Proverbs 15:33 NIV says Wisdom's instruction is to fear the Lord, and humility comes before honor. my late grandfather would say your gifts will take you places and open doors of opportunity, but your character will keep you there, if your character is not good and you just have a bad attitude and a mean demeanor all the time you have a problem and you are the problem. humble yourself under the mighty hand of God and be clothed with humility and the Lord will exalt you in due season. allow the word of God to work in you so that your transformation will take place. God will put us through test to humble us [Deuteronomy 8].

[6] To be stable in God we must study and meditate upon the word of God [John1:1] [2 Timothy 2:15 NIV says; Study to shew thyself approve unto God, a workman that needeth not to be ashamed, rightly dividing the word of truth. Hebrews 4:12 NIV says; the word of God is alive and active. Sharper than any double-edged sword, it penetrates even to dividing soul and spirit, joints and marrow; it judges the thoughts and attitudes of the heart. Knowing the word of God and using it in prayer is a powerful weapon against the enemy. Ephesians 6:17 AMP says, and take

the Helmet of salvation, and the sword of the spirit, which is the WORD OF GOD. The word of God is a part of your armor in God it is powerful and effective against the adversary.

[7] To be stable in God <u>we need spiritual wisdom</u> James 1:5 NIV says; if any of you lacks wisdom, you should ask God who gives generously to all without finding fault, and it will be given to you. These are some scriptures you can meditate upon. Proverbs 2:6, James 3:17, Proverbs 16:16, Proverbs 13:10, Proverbs 19:8,1Corinthians 3:18, Ephesians 5:15-16, Proverbs 16:16, Proverbs 19:8.

John 6:35 NIV then Jesus declared, "I am the bread of life. Whoever comes to me will never go hungry, and whoever believes in me will never be thirsty.

James 5:16 KJV says, confess your faults one to another, and pray one for another, that ye may be healed. The effectual fervent prayer of a righteous man availeth much. Prayer is a key.

What is prayer?

Prayer is having an open communication or conversation with our heavenly father with sincerity and reverence making petition and supplication unto him submitting to a higher power and Authority with thanksgiving and praise and pouring out our affections to the lord. It is also our act of faith in God. prayer is also Making our request be known and declaring what is already done in the heavens to manifest in the earthly realm and seeking answers and direction on the path that we should take. (Philippians 4:6-7 Niv) do not be anxious about anything, but in every situation, by prayer and petition with thanksgiving, present your request to God And the peace of God which transcends all understanding will guard your hearts and minds in Christ Jesus. You sometimes may not have the right words to say in prayer or you may feel like you're not eloquent in speech but it's not about how well you can speak or cannot speak because our heavenly father understands each of us, he sees what is on our hearts and knows our thoughts, there is nothing hidden from him. One thing he ask is for us to come boldly. we must be honest in prayer he said come boldly to the throne of grace where we can find mercy and help in times of need (Hebrews 4:16 NIV) Come onto him with your burdens your concerns your worries your afflictions your mistakes come to him when you are feeling down and confuse and are tried of been tried when you are face with issues that seem difficult to solve he is a problem solver, he is a friend that sticks closer than a brother, he is a way maker when there seem to be no way, a burden bearer a comforter when you're in need of comfort, he is a father to the fatherless, a Doctor when you are sick and in need of healing he is a healer, he is our protection when we are in need of being protected, he is mighty in battle he is our battle axe how great is our God he is great and greatly to be praise Emanuel!!! the God that is with us. sometimes you may not have any words to say to him just exalt him, David exalts him.

Psalms 117:1-2 NIV Praise the lord, all you nation; extol him, all you, people. For great is his love toward us, and the faithfulness of the lord endures forever. Praise the lord.

Psalms 108: 1-5 NIV my heart, O God, is steadfast, I will sing and make music with all my soul. Awake, harp and lyre! I will awaken the dawn. I will praise you, lord, among the nations; I will sing of you among the people for great is your love, higher than the heavens; your faithfulness reaches to the skies. Be exalted, o God above the heavens; let your glory be over all the earth.

sometimes you can just sit or laydown before him in silent open your heart to him and listen to what he has to say to you. When you are in a relationship or marriage, there must be proper communication for it to work out or for both of you to accomplish anything. proper Communication is very important. Now that you are in a covenant relationship with God Praying, fasting, studying and meditation on the word of God It is the foundations of which our relationship with our heavenly father is built upon. he says study to show thyself approve, knowing is word is knowing him on a different level. In the beginning was the word and the word was with God and the word was God.

Deuteronomy 6:5-8 NIV) love the lord your God with all your heart and soul and with all your strength. These commandments that I give you today are to be on your hearts. Impress them on your children. Talk about them when you sit at home and when you walk along the road, when you lie down and when you get up.

To be consistent in intercessory prayer you must fully submit yourself to the holy spirit, that when the holy spirit wakes you up at night or during the daytime to pray you are ready to do so. sometimes the holy spirit will come up on you and gives you the unction to pray be obedient to the unction of the holy spirit. it will take the love you have for the lord and commitment to him and in him to walk in obedience. it takes patience, acceptance of who you are and who he is to you. (His he your friend your lord and savior or just your provider? Prayer will draw you closer and closer to him you will feel a sense of security and strength knowing that he is in control, the lord God almighty is in control of everything in our lives and when you have come to an acceptance of that you will commit your lives to him more and more each day. prayer opens an awareness to the spiritual realms and grant you access to spiritual blessings it gives you clarity. Spending time in prayer becomes personal to us it is kneeling and talking to our creator our master and the king of kings in reverence surrounded by unconditional love. prayer gives us a sense of peace and stability. Prayer has a way of humbling us from being prideful and let us see things in the natural and spiritually in a different way than usual. As we pray, we are drawn closer to him it deepens our relationship with him and it opens our spiritual eyes and ears and keep us connected in the spiritual realm. the presence of Lord brings us comfort and relieves us of life issues. Matthew 11:28-30 Niv Jesus says comes to me, all you who are weary and burdened, and I will give you rest. Take my yoke upon you and learn from me, for I am gentle and humble in heart, and you will find rest for your soul. For my yoke is easy and my burden is light. Prayer brings and keeps us in the presence of the Lord we get encouragement in prayer, and it fortifies us, it forms an edge of protection around us and around the things that concerns us. Thank you, Lord,

Psalms 91-1-2 NIV says; whoever dwells in the shelter of the most high will rest in the shadow of the almighty. I will say of the lord, he is my refuge and fortress, my God, in whom I trust.

David when in distress because of his enemies cry out to the lord.

Psalms 102:1-2 NIV Hear my prayer, lord; let my cry for help come to you. Do not hide your face from me when I am in distress. Turn your ears to me; when I call, answer me quickly.

Psalms 123 KJV unto thee lift up mine eyes, o thou that dwellest in the heavens. Behold, as the eyes of servants look unto the hand of their masters, and as the eyes of a maiden unto the hand of her mistress; so, our eyes wait upon the lord our God, until that he have mercy upon us. Have mercy upon us: for we are exceedingly filled with contempt. Our soul is exceedingly filled with the scorning of those that are at ease, and with the contempt of the proud.

Psalms 109: 1-5 NIV my God, whom I praise, do not remain silent, for people who are wicked and deceitful have opened their mouths against me; they have spoken against me with lying tongues. With words of hatred they surround me; they attack me without cause. In return for my friendship, they accuse me, but I am a man of prayer. They repay me evil for good, and hatred for my friendship.

There are times in our lives as we walk with the Lord that we will be under attack by enemies or foes, and we will at times go before the lord in anguish and pain sometimes it become overwhelming because in those moment our human nature is waring against our spiritual man and remember that we are spirit being living in an earthly body. so, in those moments there is a war going on in our flesh because the flesh wants to do what it wants to do. and There are times when we must pray some violent prayer because we are on the battlefield. We are solders in the army of the lord David said in that same scripture (Psalms 109 NIV) may the accusers prayers condemn him may his days be few; may his children be fatherless and his wife a widow. May his children be wandering beggars; may they be driven from their homes. May a creditor seize all he has; may strangers plunder the fruits of his labor. May no one extend kindness to him or take pity on his fatherless children. David was not playing with is adversaries. Some believers in the body of Christ may say well we need to pray for them because the word says we must pray for those who despitefully use us and say all manner of evil against you falsely let God judge them. But can I say, and I quote this passage; there is a time and a season for everything under the heavens (Ecclesiastes 3NIV) the bible also says from the days of John the baptism, the kingdom of heaven suffered violence, and the violent take it by force. (Matthew 11:12 KJV) we cannot be passive when the enemy revolt against us. David says in

Psalms 35 NIV content, lord, with those who content with me; fight against those who fight against me. Take up shield and armor; arise and come to my aid. Brandish spear and javelin against those who pursue me.

Psalms 27: 1-5 NIV the lord is my light and my salvation- whom shall, I fear? The lord is the stronghold of my life- of whom shall I be afraid? WHEN THE WICKED advance against me to devour me, it is my enemies and foes who will stumble and fall, though an army besiege me, my heart will not fear; though war break out against me, even then I will be confident. One thing I ask from the lord, this only do I seek: that I may dwell in the house of the lord all the days of my life, to glaze on the beauty of the lord and to seek him in his temple. For in the days of trouble he will keep me safe in his dwelling; he will hide me in the shelter of his sacred tent and set me high upon a rock.

1Samuel chapter 17. when the Philistine champion Goliath came up against Israel, David a shepherd boy stood up against him when everyone was terrified of him. David went out to him and said who is this uncircumcised philistine that he should defy the armies of the living God? There are giants we must face in our lives that we must be brave, bold and without fear knowing that God is with us, David stood up against Goliath with a sling and a stone without a sword in his hand he struck down goliath and when he fell David took his sword after he kill him and cut his head off. There are some giants that we must face that we cannot be passive because the enemy is not playing, he has no mercy, and he does not play fair he does not care who you are or what ethnicity or background you are from, the devil has one agender to destroy you. giants do die the bigger they are the harder they fall. What looks like a giant before us is nothing in the sight of God. we can say to the mountains in our lives be thou remove and be cast into the sea, and it will be done the same way if you're facing your giants with faith giant can be destroyed in Jesus' name.

I was face with a certain situation, and One day I was having a conversation with my sister and (this is my sister's way of telling me do not play with the enemy and to fight back) she said to me sis you cannot put the enemy into a stroller like a baby and sing lullaby to him, or to the situation that you are facing, meaning the tricks, device and schemes of the adversary the devil, she was saying to me that when we are face with attacks from the enemy we cannot be passive, compassionate or show any kind of weakness, because the enemy will prey on you and A lot of times we do so because we were taught to let God fight our battle, yes God will fight our battles but there are some battle that requires our participation because God has given us dominion in the earth. We must keep in mind that the enemy has no mercy towards us and at times we allow him or is devices to overpower us and back us into a corner like we are powerless, but we are not powerless, because greater is he that is in you and in me than he that is in the world. We must be radical in our walk with God because the devil doesn't play fair he wants to steal, kill, and destroy. He doesn't just want to leave you with a black eye he wants to pluck that eye out. One thing we can be certain of is that God is with us. And he will not allow the enemy to destroy you and I if we are in right standing with him but each one of us has a part to play in the kingdom of God play your part and leave the rest to the Lord.

Paul an apostle of Jesus Christ says in Romans 8:38-39 NIV for I am convinced that neither death nor life, neither angels nor demons, neither the present nor the future, nor any powers, neither height nor depth, nor anything else in all creation, will be able to separate us from the love of God that is in Christ Jesus our lord. We have an anchor my brothers and sisters in Christ Jesus.

If we walk the path that he has set out for each and everyone of us, obey his commands, keep his precepts and his ordinances, cloth ourselves with humility God's anchor holds despite of the storm. The love that God has for us stands strong than anything this world can ever offer us, the word of God says for God so love the word that he gave his only begotten son that whosoever believe in him should not perish but have everlasting life John 3:16 NIV. he sent not is son into the world not to condemn the world but that the world might be save through him. My prayer for you today is that if you do not know the lord as your personal savior that you will take the first step today and accept him has your Lord and savior it's simple just asking him to forgive you for all your sins and open your heart to him. The bible says if any man be in Christ, he is new creature old things are passed away and behold all things become new. 2 Corinthians 5:17 KJV. to Walk in the newness of life it will take a made-up mind. Going to church every Sunday does not mean that we are there, the life we live in God is what leads us into the newness of life. If we would just take steps each day to be more and more like him and submit our body, soul, and spirit to him so that he can mold us into what he wants us to be and lead us into what he has called us to do for him. his will must be done in our lives in Jesus mighty name.

I pray today in the mighty name of Jesus Christ that his will be done in your lives in Jesus mighty name. and that you will remain faithful unto him just as he is faithful towards us. Having a prayer life is one of the most rewarding, precious, and sacred time in our lives when we can commune with the king of kings and the lord of lords it is a privilege and an honor.

2Chronicle 6,7 NIV; after Solomon build the temple for the lord he went before the lord in prayer and supplication for the people and he dedicated the temple to the lord and make is request known unto the lord. after he had prayed fire came down from heaven and consume the burnt offering and sacrifice. When the people saw this, they knelt on the pavement with their faces to the ground, and they worshiped and gave thanks to the lord. The lord appeared to Solomon at night and said to him I have heard your prayers. We as people of God must alien ourselves to the purposes of God so that when we call upon the lord, we will get his attention, and he will come to see about us.

The lord said to Solomon if my people that are call by my name would humble themselves and pray and seek my face and turn from there wicked ways, then I will hear from heaven, and I will forgive their sin and will heal their land. 2 Chronicles 7:14 NIV.

If we do not pray heaven cannot respond. If we humble ourselves turn from our wicked ways and pray heaven responds to our prayers and supplications unto the lord. He said if my people. The ones that carry is name that have the mark the set apart ones humble themselves and pray and seek his face he will forgive us of our sins and answer our prayers, that is an instruction from the lord that we need to follow. It's not only an instruction but a command. If you will do that then I the lord will do this. We need healing. Our communities need healing the word of God says we all have sin and come short of the glory of God. sin is always at our doors, and we open the door in many ways and let sin in knowingly and unknowingly sin is sin. We cannot allow sin to take up residents in our lives or allow the adversary to use our bodies as an instrument for his works [Romans 6:13 NIV]. But we are to present our body as instrument to God for his glory. and that's why repentance should be our daily prayers for us to be in right standing with God. Our sin can be a blockage, a hinderance a stumbling block between us and our heavenly father. James 5:16 NIV says; therefore, confess your sins to each other and pray for each other so that you may be healed the prayer of a righteous person is powerful and effective. If we are not walking in righteousness our prayer cannot be effective. If we are not obedient to the word of God, we will not be in right standing with God he said obedient is better than sacrifice and disobedience is as of witchcraft. When Saul disobeyed the order of the lord in 1Samuel 15 KJV the lord said to him go destroy these wicked people, the Amalekites; wage war against them until you have wiped them out because of what they did to Israel when they came up out of Egypt; But Saul did not complete the command of the lord he bring back Agag the king. The solders took sheep and cattle from the plunder to sacrifice to God but Samuel the prophet say to Saul does the lord delight in burnt offerings and sacrifices as much as in obeying the lord? To obey is better than sacrifices, and to heed is better than the fat of a rams. For rebellion is like the sin of divination, and arrogance like the evil of idolatry. Because you rejected the word of the lord, he has rejected you as king.

And just like that the lord took away the kingship from Saul. being Disobedient, murmuring and complaining are not to be taken lightly it can cause destruction to come upon us as well as things being delayed. it can stop the promises that God has for us, perfect example the children of Israel what should have taken them days took them years and many of them died, our ways must be pleasing to God. In (numbers 14 NIV) because of the grumbling against Moses and Aaron the lords anger kindle against his own people Israel and the same person they were murmuring against had to intervene on their behalf the lord wanted to just destroy them but Moses plead and remind the lord of his own words, a lot of us need to repent in this very moment for murmuring and complaining each and every day it has become a bad habit and it is a sin, Philippians 2:14 KJV do all things without murmurings and disputing. Proverbs 19:3 KJV) the foolishness of man perverteth his way: and his heart fretteth against the lord. Let us give thanks unto the lord for he is good, and his mercy endure forever let us give thanks unto the lord for he is a merciful God we must thank God each day for the cross and the blood that was shed for us all. Because of the Israel rebellion those who came out of Egypt did not enter the promise land except Joshua and Caleb. the lord said not one of them who saw my glory and the sighs I performed in Egypt and in the wilderness but who disobeyed me and tested me ten times-not one of them will ever see the land I promised on oath to their ancestors. No one who treated me with contempt will ever see it. We must go by God's ordinances and precepts they still stand as a guide in our lives in him. Proverbs 3:1-2 KJV says; my son, forget not my laws; but let thine heart keep my commandments: for length of days, and long life, and peace, shall they add to thee. Ecclesiastes 12:13 KJV; let us hear the conclusion of the whole matter: for God and keep his commandments: for this is the whole duty of man. May our desire be to please our heavenly father.

Matthew 6:5-13NiV) And when you pray, do not be like the hypocrites, for they love to pray standing in the synagogues and on the street corner to be seen by others. Truly I tell you, they have received their reward in full. but when you pray, go into your room, close the door, and pray to your father, who unseen. Then your father, who sees what is done in secret, will reward you. And when you pray, do not keep on babbling like pagans, for they think they will be heard because of their many words. Do not be like them, for your father knows what you need before you ask him. This then, is how you pray:

Our father in heaven, hallowed be your name, your kingdom come, your will be done, on earth as it is in heaven. Give us today our daily bread. And forgive us our debts, as we also have forgiven our debtors. And lead us not into temptation but deliver us from the evil one.

Being a part of the body of Christ and attending a few churches I observe and come to the realization that prayer meetings are not prioritize has much as it should be in some of the ministries today. The shut-in prayer overnight or 5am where we all come together and pray corporately. we can never pray too much, communication with the Lord is never too much it is necessary. he said upon this rock I build my church and the gate of hell shall not prevail against it Matthew 16:18 KJV. he is the master builder sometimes we can forget that he is in charge. prayer meeting should be a vital part of the church schedules. I believe corporately we need to experience and communicate with God as well as privately. And so, we have people in the church for years and are afraid when they are call upon to pray corporately, why? they do not know how to pray because they have not seen it demonstrate to them Constantly and consistently that it may become a part of their lifestyle. Many have not come from homes that they were taught to pray or seen it demonstrate to them either. The church is a hospital and a training ground for each one of us. We are all sick people in need of healing, restoration, transformation, comfort, forgiveness, genuine love, and a peace of mind.

Matthew 26:36-46 (NIV) then Jesus went with his disciples to a place called Gethsemane, and he said to them, "sit here while I go over there and pray." He took Peter and the two sons of Zebedee along with him, and he began to be sorrowful and trouble. Then he said to them, my soul is overwhelmed with sorrow to the point of death. Stay here and keep watch with me." Going a little farther, he fell with his face to the ground and prayed, my father, if it is possible, may this cup be taken from me. Yet not as I will, but as you will." Then he returned to his disciples and found them sleeping, because their eyes were heavy. so he left them and went away once more and prayed the third time, saying the same thing. Then he returned to the disciples and said to them "are you still sleeping and resting? Look, the hour has come, and the son of man is delivered into the hands of sinners. Rise! let us go! here comes my betrayer!"

Jesus knew what was about to take place, but he was still praying and making supplication to his father. That was the purpose for which he had come but he was still praying for it to pass from him, sometimes it will get hard but just keep pressing the road is rough but keep pressing, you may be tired and weary but keep on pressing and moving forward because God's will most be done in our lives in Jesus' name amen.

James 5:13-18 NIV Is anyone among you in trouble? Let them pray. Is anyone happy? Let them sing songs of praise. Is anyone among you sick? Let them call the elders of the church to pray over them and anoint them with oil in the name of the lord. and the prayer offered in faith will make the sick person well; the lord will raise them up. If they have sinned, they will be forgiven. therefore, confess your sins to each other so that you may be healed. The prayer of the righteous person is powerful and effective.

GLORY TO GOD!!!

The scripture says that Jesus told his disciples that they should always pray it is a command (Luke 18:1 NIV). its not a question of if we should pray, we must pray. in (Luke18 NIV) it tells us a story about a judge who neither fear God nor care what people thought and there was a widow in that town who keep coming to him with a plea to grant her justice against her adversaries for some time he refuses, but because she keeps brothering him, he said

I will see that she gets justice against her adversary. and because she was persistence, she got justice against her adversary. We must travail in prayer keep going back to God press in until we see the manifestation of what we are praying for. Pray with an expectation. (2chronicles 7 NIV) If my people, who are call by my name, will humble themselves and pray and seek my face and turn from their wicked ways, then I will hear from heaven, and I will forgive their sin and will heal their land. be Consistent in prayer and endure hardship. the word of God says (1Peter 5:10 AMP) After you have suffered for a little while, the God of all grace [who imparts his blessing and favor], who call you to his eternal glory in Christ, will himself complete, confirm, strengthen, and establish you [making you what you ought to be].

Luke 22:39-46 (NIV) Jesus went as usual to the mount of olives, and his disciples followed him. On reaching the place, he said to them. "pray that you will not fall into temptation." He withdrew about a stone's throw beyond them, knelt down and prayed, father, if you are willing, take this cup from me; yet not my will, but yours be done." And the angel from heaven appeared to him and strengthened him. And being in anguish, he prayed more earnestly, and his sweat was like drops of blood falling to the ground. when he rose from prayer and went back to the disciples, he found them asleep, exhausted from sorrow. Why are you sleeping?" he asked them. Get up and pray so that you will not fall into temptation."

We must pray that we do not fall into temptations Jesus was in anguish, but he prayed earnestly, the lord will strengthen us in prayer. in our weaknesses he gives us the strength. the bible says the angel appeared to him and give him strength in prayer, he said in his word he has command is angel charge over us to keep us. (Psalms 91:11-12 NIV) for he will command his angels concerning you to guard you in all your ways; they will lift you up in their hands, so that you will not strike your foot against a stone.

Prayer is a vital part of our spiritual journey with the almighty God. It is imperative that we pray in season and out of season. If our mouths are close, then heaven cannot move on our behalf and that is what the enemy wants us to stay in silents, be frustrated, Depress, worried, defeated, and weak, the enemies plan is for us not to walk into what God has for us to do and the blessing he has already bestowed on us. The scripture says that the Thief comes to kill to steal and to destroy but Jesus came that we may have life in abondance John 10:10 ESV. my prayer for you today is that you will take your position in God endure as a good solder press to the mark of the higher calling in Christ Jesus, open your mouth drive out demons lay your hands on the sick in Jesus' name, and they shall recover in Jesus' name. speak to the mountains that is in your way to be thou remove and cast into the sea the enemy want to trap us into thinking we have no power. But I beg to differ we have power in the name of Jesus he did not leave us powerless we have power in us. walk into your blessings in Jesus mighty name. walk into your calling look to the one who has called you. Be patient, be kind. let your light shine in the darkness in Jesus might name.

A step-by-step guide. On how to pray.

The First step is acknowledgement and worship.

You must acknowledge who he is and who you are praying to, our heavenly father who art in heaven the lord God almighty. When we walk up to some one to have a conversation, we first acknowledge the person by their name it is an act of honor, respect, politeness, humility, and it also gets their attention. and as we go before or in the presence of the king of kings and the lord of lord, we must show respect, honor, reverence, and gratitude to him our creator. Bring a sacrifice of thanksgiving, praise, exaltation, and adoration unto him. Singing spiritual songs or hymns to him. **relate back to him his word, who he is and what he meant to you making it personal or in other words intermate. For example. Lord you are my shepherd my hiding place a very help in times of trouble lord you are wonderful there is no one like you no one can touch my heart like you do without you lord I am nothing lord. I love you lord. I need you. Delight yourself in him be sincere because God sees your hearts, He deserves all our worship and honor.** Psalm 95:1- 7 NIV Come, let us sing for joy to the lord; let us shout aloud to the rock of our salvation. Let us come before him with thanksgiving and extol him with music and song. For the lord is the great god the great king above all gods.

In his hands are the depths of the earth, and the mountain peaks belong to him. the sea is his, for he made it and his hands formed the dry land.

Come, let us bow down in worship, let us kneel before the lord our maker; for he is our god, and we are the people of his pasture. The flock under his care.

The Second step is confession.

You must confess all your sins and ask the lord for forgiveness and if there is any unforgiveness in your heart ask him to help you to forgive. You can also loose yourself from unforgiveness by choosing to let go, the hurt, the offence or whatever it may be, because the word of God says if we do not forgive, he will not forgive us for our sins. Matthew 6:14-15 NKJV for if you forgive men their trespasses, your heavenly Father will also forgive you. But if you do not forgive men their trespasses, neither will your father forgive your trespasses. [You can Read; Romans 3:21-23 KJV) we all have sinned and fall short of the glory of God. Unrepented sin can block our prayers as well as being disobedient, unforgiving, and holding grudges towards someone, we must free ourselves from these sins. Being disobedient to God can cause our prayers to be block and hinder our blessings and the lord said we must forgive.

Hebrews 4:14-16 NIV Therefore, since we have a great high priest who has ascended into heaven, Jesus the son of God, let us hold firmly to the faith we confess. For we do not have a high priest who is unable to empathize with our weakness, but we have one who has been tempted in every way, just as we are- yet he did not sin. Let us then approach God's throne of grace with confidence, so that we may receive mercy and find grace to help us in our time of need.

The scripture says in 1Samuel 15:22-23 NIV, But Samuel replied Does the lord delight in burnt offerings and sacrifices as much as in obeying the Lord? to obey is better than sacrifice, and to heed is better than the fat of rams. For rebellion is like the sin of divination, and arrogance like the evil of idolatry. Because you have rejected the word of the lord, he has rejected you as king. Because of Saul's disobedience God rejected him as king.

Proverbs 28:9 NIV, if anyone turns a deaf ear to my instruction, even their prayers are detestable.

The third step is making your request and petitions.

make your request be known to him ask for what you need.

Matthew 7:7-8 (NIV) ask, and it will be given to you; seek and you will find; knock and the door will be opened to you. For everyone who asks receives; the one who seeks finds; and to the one who knocks, the door will be opened.

Philippians 4:6-7(NIV) do not be anxious about anything, but in every situation, by prayer and petition, with thanksgiving, present your requests to god. And the peace of god, which transcends all understandings, will guard your hearts and your minds in Christ Jesus.

There is also a time and season for everything under the sun and so while we are praying, we need to keep this in mind that somethings that we are praying for may not be the right time or season for it. Answers being Delay is not a denial. And it also could be warfare going on in the heavenly realms, perfect example Daniel chapter 10) the first time Daniel prayed God heard him and sent the answer, but the prince of Persia hold up the answer to Daniel's prayer there was warfare going on after Daniel prayed, the enemies job is to stop your blessing and block you from moving forward in God but I come to encourage you today push, don't stop praying until you see the manifestation of what you prayed for as you pray the will of the Father. On the other hand, could it be that the very thing that you are praying for is not in the will of our heavenly father for your life. Sometimes we as a believer can have goals for our lives and that can be a good thing, we must have goals but is it the will of God for our lives. That is why it is important to be fill with the holy spirit because the spirit make intercession for us the bible says we know not what to pray for, but the spirit knows the will of our heavenly father. the spirit also knows the time and the season that we are in.

Ecclesiastes 3:1-8 NIV there is a time for everything, and season for every activity under the heaven; a time to be born and a time to die, a time to plant and a time to uproot, a time to kill and a time to heal, a time to tear down and a time to build, a time to weep and a time to laugh, a time to mourn, and a time to dance, a time to scatter stones and a time to gather them, a time to embrace and a time to refrain from embracing, a time to search and a time to give up, a time to keep and a time to throw away, a time to tear and a time to mend, a time to be silent and a time to speak, a time to love and a time to hate, a time for war and a time for peace.

Galatians 6:8-10 NIV whoever sows to please their flesh, from the flesh will reap destruction; whoever sows to please the spirit, from the spirit will reap eternal life. Let us not become weary in doing good, for at the proper time we will reap a harvest if we do not give up. Therefore, as we have opportunity, let us do good to all people, especially to those who belong to the family of believers.

It's not for us to just pray but we must do good, treat other how we would want to be treated. whatsoever we sow we will also reap remember that we serve a God that sees all things, know all things, everything is naked before him, and he is a just God, he is not partial he deals with us accordingly.

The promises of God are sure but not everyone will see the promises of God, you may say but why would I say that? I Am glad you ask.

Hebrews11 NIV) Now faith is confidence in what we hope for and assurance about what we do not see.

In the same chapter of Hebrews 11 NIV the bible says that all these people were living by faith when they died. They did not receive the things promised; they only saw them and welcome them from a distance, admitting that they were foreigners and strangers on the earth.

Some promises will pass on to the next generation, when God use Moses to the deliver the children of Israel out of Egypt because of their disobedience some of them die in the wilderness but their children enter in the promises land, I would say then that we can forfeit the promises of God in our lives, and it pass on to our children or our children's children. Yes, we can by walking in disobedience, God took the kingship from Saul. Don't forfeit what God has for you or what God has given you. Some promises are conditional there is a clause that attached with it.

How can I pray effectively?

The scripture says in (Hebrews 11:6 KJV) and without faith it is impossible to please God, he that cometh to God must believe that he his and he is a rewarder to them that diligently seek him. We must believe when we pray it is already done. (Matthew 9:27 – 30 Niv) Jesus ask the blind men do you believe am able to do this. Yes, lord they replied then he touch their eyes and said according to your faith let it be done to you. And their sight was restored. Believe and you shall receive your healing and deliverance in Jesus mighty name. praying his word back to him is one of the tools to an effective prayer life. we most speak is word back to him. Live a life that is pleasing to God a life of holiness it is required of us to please God.

James 5:16 NIV Therefore confess your sins to each other and pray for each other so that you may be healed the prayer of the righteous is powerfully and effective. we must also have an expectation in prayer for God to speak or move on our behalf. The lord asks Ezekiel the Question in Ezekiel 37:2 NIV "Son of man can these bones live. it not that the lord does not know if the dry bones can live, it is for us to believe and use our authority in God to speak to the dead situations in our lives to come back to life and we will see the manifestation of the supernatural in our lives. Believe in him and believe that it is already done in Jesus' name. for our prayers to be effective our lifestyle must align with the word of God. we must live a consecrated and holy lifestyle.

Holiness is a command from the lord. (1Peter 1:16 NIV For it is written: "Be holy, because I am holy."

Leviticus11:45 ESV I am the lord, who brought you up out of Egypt to be your god; you shall therefore be holy, for I am holy. He told the children of Israelites they should not touch nothing that is unclean. There are stipulations, regulations, and command that God has put in place for us to follow it is all in his word. (Deuteronomy 6).

1Peter 1:14- 16 NIV as obedient children, do not conform to the evil desires you had when you lived in ignorance. But just as he who called you is holy, so be holy in all you do; for it is written:" be holy, because I am holy."

To be effective in prayer it required for you to have times of fasting. A period in which you fast and pray.

fasting is a priority it a means of cleaning the body both naturally and spiritually it eliminates dunks from our spirit and body, and it lifts our spirit to God, it empowers us spiritually, and that is the strength we need for our prayer to be effective they both go hand in hand. We must balance our fasting and prayer life not just corporately but privately. We must Read the word of God daily and meditate upon the word. Psalms 119:105 NIV says; your word is a lamp for my feet, a light on my path. watch and pray so that the enemy does not come in unaware, because we wrestle not against flesh and blood but against principality and powers against the rulers of darkness against spiritual wickedness in high places. [Ephesians

6:12 KJV]. with this in mine it is not against our brothers and sisters or friends or families, it's spiritual warfare. pray until there is a shifting in your spirit. Even your own mind at times will also have a warfare going on. There are times when I go in prayer where there is a lot of things going through my mind and I had to speak to my mind and tell it to be silent. 2 Corinthians 10:5 KJV says; Cast down imaginations, and every high thing that exalteth itself against the knowledge of God and bringing into captivity every thought to the obedience of Christ. (Romans 8:8 Niv) those who are in the realm of the flesh cannot please God. these are some of the keys or tools to an effective prayer life. The scripture says we know not what to pray for, pray in your heavenly language the spirit will make intercession for us. Can I also share a little secret with you the more you pray is the more the enemy comes after you to distract you from your purpose but do not be afraid the scripture says when the enemy comes in like a flood the spirit of the lord will lift a standard against what every he throws at you. when you are a threat to the enemy's camp, he will always try to take you out or bring distraction even through the people that are close to you. but God will not allow him to take you out the scripture says in Isaiah 54:17 KJV) the weapon will form but it cannot prosper. Endure as good solders. Jesus endures the cross and we have his spirit living on the inside of us. Greater his he that is in you than he that is in the world.

2Timothy2:11-13(NIV) If we died with him, we will also live with him; if we endure, we will also reign with him, if we disown him, he will also disown us; if we are faithless, he remains faithful, for he cannot disown himself.

Daniel got down on his knees and prayed three times a day. for our prayer to be effective it takes commitment, self-control, self-discipline, and perseverance. the enemy will try to attack your prayer life. they plot against Daniel. the bible says that Daniel had exceptional qualities, so the king planned to set him over the whole kingdom. When you are about to be elevated the enemy will show up, he is the accuser of the brethren. And he will use the people around you even the closes ones to you. they all plot against Daniel they were strategic in plotting against him, they said (Daniel 6 NIV) they could not find no corruption in him or any grounds to charge him, so they went after his prayer life his relationship with God. They said we will never find any basis for charges against this man Daniel unless it has to do with the law of his God." So, they conspire together then went to the king maliciously against Daniel. I could say that they manipulate the king, or you could say they deceive the king, people will go at any length to try and stop or block you from walking into your blessings. But be steadfast in prayer don't relent for praying. One of the things that I see in this chapter of Daniel 6 NIV is that the word said he had a good conduct, and he was trustworthy they could find no negligent or corruption in the position he was in. even the angel when he appeared to Daniel said you who are highly esteemed. we are accountable for our conduct both spiritual and when we are on our circular jobs the enemy will look for any door to invade our lives and bring accusations against us, but we are to walk circumspect before the almighty God, so the enemy has no grounds to operate. and although they plot against Daniel that did not stop Daniel from praying, he prayed and ask the lord for help. When we find ourselves in difficult situations that is when we should pray even more, press into prayer. Prayer is an effective tool for the children of God our prayers can move the hands of God to work on our behalf.

Don't be selfish in prayer, pray for the people of God pray for the nation, your community and don't just pray for your children pray for the child next door or those in your region pray for the single mothers and fathers you see that are struggling with their children, pray for the teachers who are teaching our children pray for the president pray for leaders' pastors, governors, senators, mayors those who are in position over us why? They are making decisions that will affect each one of us and the word of God says we should pray for them. our prayers need to go beyond our household so we may live peacefully.

1Timothy 2 NIV I urge, then, of all, that petitions, intercession, and thanksgiving be made for all people- for kings and all those in authority, that we may live peaceful and quiet lives in all godliness and holiness. This is good, and pleases God our savior, who wants all people to be saved and to come to a knowledge of the truth. For there is one God and one mediator between God and mankind, the man Christ Jesus, who give himself as a ransom for all people.

when Daniel understood from the scriptures, according to the word of the lord given to Jeremiah the prophet that the desolation of Jerusalem would last seventy years and the vision he got. Daniel fast and pray and plead to the lord. The bible says while Daniel was speaking and praying, confessing is sin and the sin of the people Israel Gabriel show up to Daniel he said to Daniel I have come to give you insight and understanding. It is through Prayer that we get clarity, the answers that we are searching for and it brings us on the right path that God has predestine for us. Our prayers should be bigger than just our needs it should include declaring in the earth realm the purposes and plans of God. Our lack of faith determines our altitude in God without faith it is impossible to please God he that cometh to God must believe that he is, and he is a rewarder to those who diligently seek him. Daniel prayed three times a day even when they plot against him and the decree was issue that the next thirty days anyone who prays to any God or human being except to you, your majesty would be thrown into the lion's den. the bible says Daniel still prayed he did not change is routine he was not afraid what man can do to him, a lot of believers are people pleasers, but when you please man you dishonor God. Our ways must please our heavenly father first. They throw Daniel in the lion's Den, but God send his angel to deliver him. Then the king issues a decree that in every part of his kingdom people must fear and reverence the God of Daniel. For he is the living God, and he endures forever; his kingdom will not be destroyed, his dominion will never end. He rescues and saves; he performs signs and wonders in the heavens and on the earth. He has rescued Daniel from the power of the lions. Your trials and tribulations will bring glory to God if you persevere to the end.

Psalms 37: 3- 6 NIV) Trust in the lord and do good; dwell in the land and enjoy safe pasture. Take delight in the lord, and he will give you the desires of your heart. Commit your way to the lord; trust in him and he will do this: he will make your righteous reward shine like the dawn, your vindication like the noonday sun.

Nehemiah 1, 2 NIV says; when he found out those who survived the exile and are back in the province are in great trouble and disgrace and the wall of Jerusalem is broken down, and the gates have been burned with fire." Nehemiah wept for some days he mourned and fasted and prayed before the lord. Not only did he prayed but he found favor in the sight of the king because God hands were upon him. He did something about what he heard and ask for assistant, when you are going to do something for the lord, he will send help pray that God will send your helper to do his will. Anything that you're going to do for God will is not going to be easy there is always a Sanballat and Tobiah to oppose the work of the lord, Ezra 4 NIV says when they were building back the temple of the lord the enemies of Judah and Benjamin heard and try to join them, but

Zerubbabel, Joshua and the rest of the heads of the Israel dismiss them that they will have no part in the building of the house of the lord, so they set out to discourage the people of Judah and make them afraid to go on building the house of the lord. Opposition will come when you are doing something that is bigger than you and that will bring glory to the almighty God, but pray, act upon his word, and press through it, God will send your helpers, kingdom builders. I pray your destiny helpers will show up in your direction in Jesus mighty name

Ezra the Priest (Ezra 9 NIV) when he saw that the people of Israel, disobey the word of the lord, they were told not to mingle with the people with their detestable practices. In Ezra 9:11-12 NIV Says, and I cote; the land you are entering to possess is polluted by corruption of its peoples they have filled it with their impurity from one end to the other therefore, do not give your daughters in marriage to their sons. Do not seek a treaty of friendship with them at any time, that you may be strong and eat the good things of the land and leave it to your children as an everlasting inheritance. but they disobey. they broke God command. including the priests and Levites, mingle the holy race with the people around them the Canaanites, Hittites, Perizzites, Jebusites, Ammonites, Moabites, Egyptians, and Amorites. They have taken some of their daughters as wives for themselves and their sons and the leaders and officials have led the way in this unfaithfulness." Ezra tore his tunic and cloak, pulled hair from his head and beard, and sat down appalled. Then Ezra fell on his knees and prayed to the lord.

Whatever affect the church and the people of God affects us we are apart of the body. Ezra saw the transgression of the people. they were given instruction not to mingle with these people and they disobeyed the lord.

after Ezra prayed the people take heed and turn from their disobedience, they put away their wives.

The lord just needs one righteous person to stand in a community, a city, a town, a village, a state, a nation, and pray and petition on behalf of his people. If my people that are call by my name would humble themselves and pray and turn from their wicked ways, then I will hear from heaven forgive their sins and heal their land. your voice can make a difference, stand up for righteousness stand up for holiness stand up when it is not popular stand up when you have no one supporting you for the cause of Christ. sometimes you will stand alone. But remember that God is always with us. In 1 kings 18 Elijah stands up against eight hundred and fifty false prophets on mount Carmel four hundred and fifty from Baal and four hundred from Asherah with no fear. Are you the one? Yes, you are. do not count out yourself greater is he that is in you than he that is in the world. when Zacchaeus the tax collector a wealthy man heard that Jesus was passing by, he climbs up into the sycamore tree just to take a glimpse of Jesus because Zacchaeus was short in statue, but Jesus calls on him Zacchaeus come down am coming to your house today Luke 19. you are the one that God is looking for. The ones that people say will never make it, the one that they say is not good enough, the cast away sinners the unqualify by men's opinions Jesus did not come for the righteous but sinners to repentance Can I encourage you today be courageous, be brave, be relentless knowing that God is with you even until the very end, the bible says since the first day Daniel set his mind to gain understanding and humble himself before the lord his words were heard, and the answer was sent but the angel said the prince of the Persian kingdom resisted me twenty-one days. When we humble ourselves and pray God hears our cries, petition, request, declaration and decrees of his people and he will come to our rescue.

Amos when seen a vision and heard the Judgment what God was going to do to his people Israel and their neighbors. Amos plead to the lord. And the lord relented for his judgment against the people.

When the children of Israel forgot what God had done for them they started to murmur and complain and the lord swore to them with a uplifted hands that he would make them fall in the wilderness, make their descendants fall among the nation they aroused the lord anger by their deeds and the plague broke out among them, but there was <u>one man</u> by the name of <u>Phinehas</u> that <u>stand up and intervened, and the plague was check</u> and it was credited to him as righteousness for endless generation to come Psalms 106. it took one man to stand against the judgment of God it took a righteous man, a man of honor and integrity a man that knows God, a man that stays in his presence, a man that has a fear of God. the word of God says the fear of the lord is the beginning of wisdom, a man that honors God, a man that reverence the lord. Sometimes it doesn't even take all of this but just a person that has the heart after God and the things of God. he said his thought and our thought are not the same sometimes we as believers judge people by their appearance, where they come from who's their parents, but God knows and see our hearts. God calls and use who he wants to call and use for his purpose wither you like them or not. take it up with God. We have so many mean-spirited people in the churches o yes they are everywhere they are being influence by the adversary the devil their aim is to attack, criticize and spew out not so nice words against God chosen vessel especially the one that are really sold out for God and want to see the move of God in the churches, but can I encourage you today Jesus the son of the living God was persecuted so shall we. but don't be shaken, stand firm, in who you have believe in Jesus the Christ the son of the living God. Sometimes if the true be told you can be affected by it, but trust God, pray and ask the lord to keep your heart pure before him, forgive and move on don't hold no one sin against them you are just holding yourself hostage ask the lord for help he is a friend that sticks closer than a brother. I pray that the peace of God will overtake the works of the adversary over all our lives in Jesus mighty name amen and amen. his grace is sufficient for us when we are weak, we are made strong in him it's not an easy road to travel but he has not brought us this far to leave us, he is a God of completion as long as we surrender everything to him. we must give him access to every area of our lives there are plenty of benefit in surrendering our everything to God, sometimes we want to just give him this part and that part and hold on to what we think we can manage on our own. We become self-sufficient thinking we don't need him in this area of our lives, but that should not be, we need him in every area of our lives we need him on our Jobs, we need him in our homes, we need him when we are about to make critical decisions or major decisions that can affect his purpose in our lives, we need him to guide us daily we need his insight, knowledge and wisdom, we need his comfort and sometimes we need his correction. we need him when we walk through the door every morning not knowing if we are going to make it back home, because tomorrow is not promise to no one, we must know that it is only by his grace why we are still here. many have pass away during the pandemic my condolences to those we have lost their loved ones, but we are still here to give him the honor, the glory and the praise in Jesus name it could have been you and I, but we have a chance to make it right with God knowing that earth is temporary, who can only have eternal life through Jesus Christ we want to make heaven our home. We all have sin and come short of the glory of God. We have a sinful nature.

Moses intervenes on behalf of the children of Israel when God told him to come up to the mountain, in Moses absents the people made an idol cast in the shape of a calf and God saw it and told Moses, his anger kindled against them he wanted to destroy them, but Moses plead with the lord on their behalf not to destroy them and the lord listen to Moses and relented. But when Moses went down off the mountain and saw what they were doing he Got hungry and broke the table that God gave him with the commandment.

Sometimes we forget where the Lord has taken us from and the things he has deliver us from, we easily forget at time let us be truthful you may say o no that's not me I always remember what God did for me, but have you ever been in a storm and you become fearful of what's going to happen is this going to work out in my favor, you forget that the lord brought you out of the last one and it is the Lord that will deliver you out of this one because he is a deliverer. The bible says many are the afflictions of the righteous, but the lord delivers them out of them all Psalm 34:19 KJV. It is in prayer that we will find comfort and strength during our afflictions. Tears is a language that God understands sometimes you do not have words to say but your tears speak for you. Abel's blood cry out when he was slayed by his brother Cain.

Palms 88 NIV David says day and night I cry out to you. May my prayer come before you; turn your ears to my cry, I am overwhelmed with troubles and my life draw near to death I am counted among those who go down to the pit; I am like one without strength.

We need to be open in prayer when we go before the lord don't be cute or macho, humble yourself, we need the Lord to intervene on our behalf. It does not matter who you are, a Baptist, an Anglican, a Presbyterian, a Catholic, or you go to a Pentecostal church, etc. it does not matter what denomination you are from, we all can have a relationship with God through prayer. Its about relationship with our creator, we must love one another, one God and the creator of all living things.

Lots life was spared because of Abraham when God was about to destroy the city of Sodom and Gomorrah.

THESE ARE PRAYER TIMES THAT WILL KEEP YOU IN THE PRESENCE OF THE LORD AND DESMANTLE THE PLOTS AND PLANS OF THE ENEMY AND KEEP YOU IN alignment with God AND BRINGS RESULTS.

3AM, 6am, 5AM, 9AM,12 NOON, 3pm, 9pm, 12 MIDNIGHT,

Because of life circumstances and schedules time has become our master, you must get here and there on time and so believers sometimes just barely have time to pray which should not be but if we make time to sacrifice it to the lord, he will also make a way for us. We are to seek the kingdom first and everything else will be added unto us, if you are on your Job at lunch time or break just take a moment and slip in a corner, restroom, in your car and say a word of prayer to the lord no one has to hear or know that you are praying but the lord. Hannah was in the temple praying and Eli the priest observing her mouth, but Hannah was praying in her heart, and her lips was moving but her voice was not heard Eli thought she was drunk. 1Samuel1:12-14. Praying in public quietly people will look at you like something is wrong with you but don't be distracted by people's opinion keep your focus on the Lord.

Matthew 6:6-8(NIV) But when you pray, go into your room, close the door, and pray to your father, who is unseen. Then your father, who sees what is done in secret, will reward you. And when you pray, do not keep babbling like pagans for they think they will be heard because of their many words. do not be like them, for your father knows what you need before you ask him. Developing a prayer life requires sacrifice to the Lord you must be strategic in prayer sometimes pray in your heart not aloud because at times there are monitoring spirit lurking around to work contrary to what you are praying for or praying about, the adversary.

Can I make you feel just a little guilty, if you are the one keep making excuses, that you have no time to spend in prayer and fasting if you love him, you will make time for the lord. Sometimes we put our time into everything else and neglect to spend time with the lord. Am sure we want God attention when we pray, and sometime God need our attention also, so he creates circumstances and situations to get us in his presence and get us on the right path. Some of us lives are not normal, we must stay in the presence of the lord, to much is given much is require of us I made a vow to the lord that every year I would take sometime out to lock myself away for two days just to seek him and bask in his presence. You cannot say you do not have the time because you take vacations and out of that time you can give the lord some time in his presence. It is through praying, fasting, and seeking the face of the Lord that you will receive power from on high. Prayerlessness cause deficiency in our spiritual life.

The prayer of a righteous person is powerful and effective, Elijah was a human being, even as we are. He prayed earnestly that it would not rain, and it did not rain on the land for three and a half years. And again, he prayed, and the heavens gave rain, and the earth produced its crops. (James 5 NIV).

Elijah prayed earnestly (it means) sincere and intense conviction; seriously.

Elijah prayed with power and authority. When we are in our rightful position in God, and we understand real authority our prayers will be effective. there is life and death in the power of our tongue, and we are made in his image and likeness and the authority that has been given unto us is to demonstrate the power of God in the earth, so man may know of a fact that the God we serve is powerful and mighty he rules the universe. Jehovah is in control of everything. the earth belongs to him, to God be the glory!

Palms 24:1-2 NIV says; the earth is the lord's and everything in it, the world, and all who live in it; for he founded it on the seas and established it on the waters.

Psalms 95:2-5 NIV let us come before him with thanksgiving and extol him with music and song for the lord is the great God, the great king above all gods. In his hands are the depts of the earth, and the mountain peaks belong to him. The sea is his, for he made it, and his hands formed the dry land.

A life without prayer is a life of emptiness, uncertainty, unrest and with no direction. Jeremiah 33:3NIV says; come to me and I will answer you and tell you great and unsearchable things you do not know. Prayer gives us access to things God wants us to know. Every plant need water and sunlight for it to grow and blossom, it is essential for the plants, without sun and water it will die at first it dries up and then starts to shrink being in his presence is a source of water and sunlight. There is spiritual growth when we stay in his presence consistently, he is our source for growth. Remember that everything you have is because of him, the breath we breathe is because of him.

Psalms 1: 1-3 NIV blessed is the one who does not walk in step with the wicked or stand in the way that sinners take or sit in the company of mockers, but whose delight is in the law of the lord, and who meditates on his Law Day and night. That person is like a tree planted by streams of water, which yields its fruit in season and whose leaf does not wither-whatever they do prospers. Jesus said to the lady at the well I can give you living water that you will never thirst again. Come let us drink from the well that will never run dry which is in Christ Jesus. Hallelujah!

Romans 12:12 NIV says; be joyful in hope, patient in affliction, faithful in prayer.

Colossians 4: 2 NIV says; Devote yourself to prayer, being watchful and thankful.

Ephesians 6:18 NIV says; take the helmet of salvation and the sword of the spirit, which is the word of God. And pray in the spirit on all occasions with all kinds of prayers and requests. With this in mind, be alert and always keep on praying for all the lord's people.

Psalms 5:1-3 NIV says; listen to my words, lord, consider my lament. Hear my cry for help, my king, and my God, for to you I pray. In the morning, lord you hear my voice; in the morning I lay my requests before you and wait expectantly.

How do I pray the will of God over my life?

In Matthew 6 NIV the word of God says, your kingdom come your will be done on earth as it is in heaven., it is already established in the heavenly's, but we have to pray by the spirit, so it come down in the earthly realm. Romans 8:5NIV says; those who live according to the flesh have their minds set on what the flesh desires; but those who live in accordance with the spirit have their minds set on what the spirit desires. The word of God says we know not what to pray for, but the spirit will make intercession for us with groanings. The spirit knows his will for our lives.

Romans 12:1-2 NIV Therefore I urge you, brothers, and sisters, in view of God's mercy to offer your bodies as a living sacrifice, holy and pleasing to God- This is your true and proper worship. Do not conform to the pattern of this world but be transformed by the renewing of your mind. Then you will be able to test and approve what Gods will is – his good, pleasing, and perfect will.

Seeking The Lord

2CHRONICLES 7:14 NIV] IF MY PEOPLE, WHO ARE CALLED BY MY NAME, WILL HUMBLE THEMSELVES AND PRAY AND SEEK MY FACE AND TURN FROM THEIR WICKED WAYS, THEN I WILL HEAR FROM HEAVEN, AND I WILL FORGIVE THEIR SIN AND HEAL THEIR LAND.

There is a difference in praying and seeking the lord. Praying is going to him with request, in intercession, in repentance, for guidance, looking for answers and declaring what is already done in the heavens to manifest in the earth. Which is of necessity. but seeking lord is a whole different level. Seeking the lord is a yearning and desire for more of him without any conditions or motives. It's where we get to a place where we just want to know him in all his spender and his glory, it become a personal pursuit seeking after him, I want to sop with you lord I want my thought to be alien with your thoughts and your ways to be my ways and your will to be my will. I need more of you Lord. It's a total surrendering of your will and your agender to conform to him in the beauty of his holiness and the loving care of his hands.

In Exodus 33:18-23 NIV then Moses said, "now show me your glory." And the lord said, "I will cause all my goodness to pass in front of you, and I will proclaim my name, the lord, in your presence. I will have mercy on whom I will have mercy and will have compassion on whom I will have compassion. But "he said, "you cannot see my face, for no one may see me and live." Then the lord said, there is a place near me where you may stand on a rock, when my glory passes by, I will put you in a cleft in the rock and cover you with my hand until I have pass by. Then I will remove my hand and you will see my back; but my face must not be seen."

Moses had been in the presence of the lord, time and time again, but he needed to know him on a different level, are you hungry for more of him, Moses asks the lord to show him his glory, Moses wanted to see him in person. How many of us need more of him how many of us are searching and seeking after the things of God? And the things that concern him, when we get to that place, we will love what he loves and hate what he hates [Sin]. when we alien ourselves in him our spirit will always have a hunger and thirst for more and more of him the lord is so gracious, he will not force himself on us we are the ones that need him more in all his spender. Deuteronomy 4:7 NIV] what other nation is so great as to have the Gods near them the way the lord our God is near us whenever we pray to him? The lord said that he will never leave us nor forsake us he will be with us even until the very end.

Philippians 3:10-11 NIV says; I want to know Christ -yes, to know the power of his resurrection and participation in his sufferings, becoming like him in his death, and so, somehow, attaining to the resurrection from the dead. Not that I have already obtained all this, or have already arrived at my goal, but I press on to take hold of that for which Christ Jesus took hold of me.

Jeremiah 29:11-14 NIV for I know the plans I have for you, declares the lord, plans to prosper you and not to harm you, plans to give you hope and a future. Then you will call on me and come and pray to me, and I will listen to you. You will seek me and find me when you seek me with all your heart. I will be found by you, declares the lord, and will bring you back from captivity. I will gather you from all the nations and places where I have banish you, declares the lord, and will bring you back to the place from which I carried you into exile.

He said if you seek me you shall find me, is he lost? No. he is not, there is a place in God where he wants us to abide spiritual but not just to abide because he takes us from glory to glory and there are different dimensions in him, there are difference levels in him. he has no limit he is limitless he cannot be measure in any capacity. he is immortal, invisible, wise beyond human measure and comprehension, he is intellectual, Moses asks him who should I tell pharaoh sent me, he said the I am. Whoever we want him to be in your lives that is who he will be in that moment, if you need to be healed he will be your healer if you need deliverance he will deliver you he is the I am, do not limit him to man's capacity of understanding of who he should be or who he is, we cannot contain him. Isaiah 55:8 NIV says; For my thoughts are not your thoughts. neither are your ways my ways declares the lord. As the heavens are higher than the earth, so are my ways higher than your ways and my thoughts than your thoughts.

Therefore, we must seek him. get in his presence. Seeking the Lord is letting go of oneself, submitting and committing our body, soul, and spirit to him in pursuit of purpose, clarity, wisdom and understanding and to know who he is, it brings change, growth and it takes the scales from our eyes and allow us to see clearer. it gives us weight in the spirit so we can carry his glory, it takes us to a spiritual altitude in him and we become a glory carrier in Jesus mighty name. seeking the Lord requires much patients and in pursuit of him, it is not for the faint of heart it is not for those who just want to settle and be saved and procrastinate. But for those we need more of him. Some of us our biggest and greatest warfare is in our mind, it is a constant battle because our mind has a voice and so sometimes if we are not careful or aware of it, we succumb to the voice of our mind that is contradictory to the voice of God. at times we have been program to think a certain way, act a certain way and at times we are being control by the strongholds of our mind. for example somethings are spiritual and somethings are natural, some of us grow up on or was brought up on a certain lifestyle, religion and culture or have been taught a certain way to do things and how we approach and handle certain situations and so we do not think outside from what we were taught or know because we have come accustom to those things, and it became hard for many of us to step outside the box, and to unlearn these habits, custom and sometimes bad behaviors that has kept us limited or restricted from transforming into the image and person that God wants us to be. If you would just step into something new. we need to change our poster. we procrastinate at times, and a lot of time fear kicks in the fear of the unknown, especially when God gives you an assignment to do and you are going somewhere you have never been before and doing something you have never done before, trying something new like going back to school to further your Education, now hear the voice in your head, your too old for school your not going to be able to retain anything it's a waste of time and money your time as past just keep working until you die or you keeping hearing the voice of someone who spoke negative words over your life it could be a parent, teacher, sibling, or someone that had or have authority over you the devil is a liar, it's never too late for progress or your dreams to come through, go ahead and open that business you have been dreaming about, go back to school make that change with God all things are possible. sometimes God is waiting for us to step in what he has already provided for us if he gives you the desires, he is able to fulfill them. Another thing that is critical in our walk with the Lord is location, some of us needs to change our location in the spiritually realm and some of us in the natural realm, we need to upgrade our walk with God when your phone need to be upgrade you go to the store and get a newly upgraded version of the phone you have, and so you need a spiritual upgrade. you have been at that level for too long it has been five, six, ten years you have been saved by the grace and mercy of God and fill with the holy spirit yet still your tongues have not change you are still a student not a teacher, all this time there is no growth you have not been baring any fruits (Hebrews 5:12-14 NIV). Let me tell you about you by the unction of the holy spirit, there is a masterpiece in you that you have not tap into has yet, greatness is in you waiting to be discovered and release, you are valuable to God he loves you with an everlasting love now get up sons and daughters of God you have been in that state long enough God's purpose is calling you and you have work to do for the kingdom of God. arise and shine for your time has come hallelujah! And the glory of God shall be revealed in your life in Jesus mighty name. there are times when God will lead you to Change your physical location sometimes God want to take you from among certain people because some of you are connected to the wrong people, so at times he will create conflicts to disconnect you from them because he wants to connect you to your destiny helpers and believers that are connected to his purpose for your life. there are places that you may go where God don't want you to go and things, he does not want you to get involve with, God knows what's best for each of us he sees far ahead and knows the outcome of a thing, those who are led by the spirit of God are the sons of God. it could be friends some of you are connected to, friends that keep on reminding you of your past and the things God has brought you out of, they sometimes want to pull you into things you have grown from and delivered from, not everyone can go where God is taking you some people are in your life for seasons and when their season is up you have to learn how to let them go. Abraham and Lot are a perfect example (Genesis 13). Sometimes God wants to remove you from that workplace to give you something better or pushing you to start your own business, to be your own boss but some of us have to get out of the Egyptian mentality and also stop being afraid to fail, but can I tell you in life you will have failure it's a must but it is a learning process for you to grow. if God tell you to do something he already made a way. God will take you out of or from your home or families wherever he sees it fit for you to go so you can be elevated and be in the right position in him for him to execute his purpose in your life. God told Abraham to leave his father's house in Genesis 12 NIV says; and God told him I the lord will make you into a great nation and bless you; I will make your name great, and you will be a blessing. the plans that God has for you he has to relocate you, make sure it is God and not the enemy wants to move you from your position to derail or divert you from the blessings that God has for you and to fulfill his purpose in your life. Walking into the unknow can become a challenge because a lot of us has an Egyptian mentality, in captivity in our mind iron bars and all, stuck and stubborn, our hearts become harden you have not allowed the word of God to break down those bars and shift your heart and your mindset, the word of God is a powerful weapon against the voice or strongholds in our mind it will reprogram your mind to the will and attributes of our heavenly father.

Hebrews 4:12 (read it).

2 Corinthians 10:5[NIV] we demolish arguments and every pretension that sets itself up against the knowledge of God, and we take captive every thought to make it obedient to Christ.

Remember whatever we think that is what we will become, never think that you are not good enough the greater one lives within you shift your focus off what you don't have and turn it to who you have been walking with the Lord, God will not leave you nor disappoint you he wants to blow your mind, the plans he have for you is great and so that he may be glorified in you and through you. May the abundance of his grace fall upon you in Jesus mighty name amen.

Psalms 27:6-9[NIV] then my head will be exalted above the enemies who surround me; at his sacred tent I will sacrifice with shouts of joy; I will sing and make music to the lord. Hear my voice when I call, lord; be merciful to me and answer me. My heart says of you, "seek his face!" your face, lord I will seek. Do not hide your face from me, do not turn your servant away in anger; you have been my helper. Do not reject me or forsake me, God my savior.

These are some of the benefits that comes from seeking the lord and staying in his presence consistently and earnestly.

Isaiah 55:6-8 AMP Seek the Lord while he may be found; call on him [for salvation] while he is near. Let the wicked leave (behind) his way and the unrighteous man his thoughts; and let him return to the Lord, and he will have compassion (mercy) on him, and to our God, for he will abundantly pardon, "For my thoughts are not your thoughts, nor are your ways my ways," declares the Lord.

Psalm 103:2-3 NIV) Praise the lord, my soul, and forget not all his benefits-who forgives all sins and heals all your diseases.

Matthew 6:33 NIV) But seek first his kingdom and his righteousness, and all these things will be given to you as well.

Psalms 111:10 NIV] the fear of the lord is the beginning of wisdom; all who follow his precepts have good understanding. To him belongs eternal praise.

A. UNMEASURABLE FAITH One of the benefits that You will receive in seeking the lord consistently is a deeper level of faith and confidence in him and in his word. And a deeper level of faith also requires for us to rest in him, rest from our own works. it's not by might, it's not by power, but by the spirit of the Lord. In earnestly and consistently seeking the lord There is no hesitation in obeying his voice when he speaks to you and give you an instruction to carry out an assignment, you will get to know his voice by being in his presence consistently. The bible says Abraham obeyed God in Genesis 22 and Genesis 12. And because he obeyed God, he become the father of many nations and his seed is blessed. We are the seed of Abraham and so we are blessed. Abraham was a friend of God. I have a Question for you can the lord call you friend? Because a friend communicates with each other consistently.

B. <u>GOD WILL POSITION YOU FOR HIS PURPOSE</u> When you seek the lord consistently and walk in obedience to him the lord will put you in position and give you the wisdom and the ability you need to do his will so that it may be done with clarity, precision and in order. It is God that gives position not man, am talking about position for the purposes of God and to do his will. when man put you in position with the wrong motives or their own agendas, they can take that position away from you when it is not profitable for them. Or for other reasons. And Sometimes the Lord will give man instruction to place you in position also for his purposes Proverbs 21:2 AMP says, Every man's way is right in his own eyes, But the Lord weighs and examines the hearts [of people and their motives]. when God put you in position no one can take you from the position God put you in. Proverbs 21: 1 KJV says; The king's heart is in the hand of the Lord, as the rivers of water: he turneth it whithersoever he will. God put Salomon in position to build the temple (1kings 6,7,8). God put Noah in position to build the ark and gave Noah instruction how to build it and Noah obeyed and did everything just as God commanded him (Genesis 6). God put Moses in position to lead the children of Israel out of Egypt and Moses did as God instructed him to do Exodus 3.10]. God put Joshua in position to lead the children of Israel into the promise land. Are you available for God to use you, have you presented you body has a living sacrifice to the Lord? in Isaiah 6:8

AMP] Then I heard the voice of the Lord, saying, "who shall I send, and who will go for us?" then I said, "here am I. send me!"

C.   GOD WILL GIVE YOU SPIRITUAL INSIGHT

seeking the lord consistently, He will give you spiritual insights and wisdom beyond what you can even imaging or think. You will gain favor in the sight of God and because you find favor with God you will find favor with man. God will send people around you that are a blessing to the called of God on your life. God gave Salomon great wisdom and insight. 1kings 3;1-28.1kings 4.

In 2 kings 6:16-22 NIV] when the army surround the city where Elisha was, his servant was in panic but Elisha prayed for the eyes of his servant to be open so he may see that there is more with them than those who were against them, and the lord open the eyes of Elisha's servant and he saw the hills full of horses and chariots of fire all around them. The eyes of Elisha servant were open When Elisha prayed, there are believers in the body that their eyes are close spiritually [spiritual blindness] and because their eyes are closed when face with opposition they panic, if you are one of them, I pray that your eyes will be open in Jesus mighty name.

D.   YOU WILL BECOME A TARGET TO THE ENEMY when you are consistent in seeking the lord, and you are walking in you assignment you will become a target and a threat to the enemies camp, you will go through spiritual warfare, attacks, persecution and sometimes the people around you will turn on you because the enemy use people that are close to you at times to distract you from focusing on the things of God especially when they are not aware of the enemies tactics. but don't stop seeking him because you are covered on every side by the lord Jesus Christ. Elijah the prophet of the lord was cover on every side 1kings 18, 1kings19. Elisha was also covered 2kings 6.

E. YOU WILL GAIN TERRITORIES AND BREAK GENERATIONAL CURSES

In seeking the lord consistently, you are breaking grounds and gaining and possessing new territories spiritually and in the natural not only for you but for your children and the next generation to come. Seeking the lord consistently there will be shifting's that take place (Exodus 33:1-3, Exodus 34:23-24) And you will gain access to an abondance of blessing both spiritual blessing and natural blessings. God told Abram I will make your name great, and you will be a blessing. (Genesis 12) We are the seed of Abram. In seeking the lord, you are becoming a trailblazer God will give you business ideas and creative ideas, you will break down barriers and door for your generation and the generations to come.

F. YOUR COUNTIANCE AND ATTITUDE WILL CHANGE

When you seek after the presence of the lord it will be evident on you and around You Exodus 34 NIV. when Moses came down from Mount Sinai after being in the presence of God, he was not aware that his face was radiant, and the people were afraid to come near him. Being in the presence of God will change your appearance, your behavior and attitude. and anywhere you go the atmosphere will change, demons will manifest themselves,

Mark 5. And even the people that you are associated with they will also see the changes in you and on you; the enemy will try to use them to distract you so you must be spiritually aware because we wrestle not against flesh and blood.

G. GOD WILL GIVE YOU A HIGH-RANKING AUTHORITY

God is looking for believers he can trust in certain positions to carry out his work and In seeking the lord faithfully, persistently and being in obedient to him, doing his will and walking into his purpose for your life, God will trust you and give you access and authority to realms in the spirit that when you pray the prayers and words that comes from your mouth becomes a sword in the enemies' camp, it will dismantle and destroy their plots and plans and overthrow demonic altars in Jesus' mighty name glory to God hallelujah! You will be able to speak to nature and they will comply to your command in Jesus' mighty name 1kings 18. This position is not to be taken lightly, when you are positioned in your assignment it is a great responsibility on you or on that person. God must put you through some trials and testing to reach at this pivotal level. in Joshua 10:1-15 NIV, Joshua told the sun to stand still over Gibeon and he said you, moon, over the valley of Aijalon." And the bible says the sun stood still and the moon stopped, till the nation avenged itself on its enemies. It is not something to be used for selfish agendas or personal gain because God will hold you or that persons responsible if you misused your authority. sometimes men and women of God lose their focus or get distracted. But always remember that God gives you high-ranking authority for his purpose and to carry out his will, sometimes men forget.

H. GOD WILL UNLOCK YOUR GIFTS AND INPART GIFTINGS IN YOU

In seeking the lord consistently and being in his presence, gifts that has been lock up in you or lay dormant in you will activate, and he will download things in your spirit meaning he will equip you for the assignment that he has for you to accomplish for his purpose, he will give you a deeper level of revelation knowledge and spiritual intelligence. And when he gives you an assignment, he will also give you instructions on how to do it and what steps to take in carrying out the assignment. (Exodus 34 NIV). Moses was on mount Sinai for 40 days and 40 nights.

Isaiah 55:6-7 NIV] seek the lord while he may be found; call on him while he is near. let the wicked forsake their ways and the unrighteous their thoughts. Let them turn to the lord, and he will have mercy on them, and to our God, for he will freely pardon.

The word of God says it is appointed unto man once to die and after death then comes judgement. We must seek him while he may be found call on him while he is near, now that we have the chance to do so don't let it be too late. Sometimes we wait until we are in trouble, make bad decision or our back is against the wall to seek or call upon the lord.

Revelation 22:12(NIV) look, I am coming soon! My reward is with me, and I will give to each person according to what they have done. I am alpha and the omega, the first and the last, the beginning and the end.

Daily Prayers

OUR FATHER WHO ART IN HEAVEN I thank you lord for today. Thank you for being a shelter for me and a strong tower from the enemy. father forgive me of all my sins and my transgressions have mercy on me lord according to your loving kindness and your tender mercy, create in me a clean heart lord and renew a right spirit in me, wash and cleans me from the crown of my head to the very soul of my feet. fill my cup lord with peace, love and joy. purge my thoughts keep my mouth from speaking guile, father help me to walk up right before you lord, because at times evil present itself and I cannot do it without you lord. Lead and guide me in the way I should take According to your word. Lord you said in your word that you have an expected end for me and so let me not lose sight of who you truly are to me. You are my keeper. my very help in time of trouble. my way maker and I love you lord, I give you all the praise in Jesus mighty name amen and amen.

Daily Prayers

Heaven father I appreciate you, I love you, I adore you; I lay my life before you father. Thank you for the breath of life. Thank you for a new day. Thank you for grace and mercy. Thank you for being patient with me lord. Forgive me of all my sins and my transgression bolt out my iniquities and my sin that is before you. And if I am walking in error father reveal it unto me lord so I can correct my ways. lord show me your way. Lead and direct me and Father thank you for being the shepherd of my life. Lord forgive me of all my sins and my transgression bolt out my iniquities and have mercy upon me. Hear my prayer o lord and come to my rescue. My total dependency is on you lord so if you do not come to my rescue, I will be lost. Sanctify me for your glory lord in Jesus mighty name.

Daily Prayer

Heavenly father hear my prayer today lord as I call on you thank you lord for another day that I can be in your presence thank you lord for keeping me in time of trouble. father forgive me lord for all my sins known and unknown things I may say or do unaware that I have sin against you, wash and cleans me with your blood lord. Father I seek your direction in _____ area of my life. I put it in your hands lord. Father I commit my life to you do as it pleases you according to Jerimiah 29:11[NIV] you said you know the plans you have for me plans to prosper me and give me a hope for the future. So, father make your path clear unto me in Jesus mighty name amen.

Daily Prayer

Lord Jesus I come before you today as humble as I know how to, father I thank you for another day I give you all the praise and all the honor in Jesus name if I have done or said anything lord that is not pleasing to you, I ask for your forgiveness, if I hold any unforgiveness in my heart against anyone I release them and release myself from unforgiveness in Jesus name, you said in your word according to Matthew 6:15[NIV] if I do not forgive others you will not forgive my sins. create in me a clean heart and renew a right spirit within me cast me not away from thy presence and please do not take your spirit from me. lord make me whole. again, Father forgive me of murmuring and complaining when you have blessed me each day. Thank you, lord, for giving me another day in Jesus' name amen.

Daily Prayer

Father who art in heaven I come to you today lord with holding nothing from you lord o wretched man that I am, father forgive me of all my transgressions and my iniquity that is so ever before you. Create in me a clean heart. and renew a right spirit within me, cast me not away from thy presence lord. I command my day to be bless in Jesus' name thank you lord for the valley experience, you said in your word that this light affliction is only for a moment and not to be compare with the glory that shall be reveal in my life. Lord give me the strength, courage, wisdom and understanding each day so I can walk into my destiny without fear and with clarity of thought in Jesus' name mighty amen.

Daily Prayer

My father in heaven I glorify your name lord you are great and greatly to be praise, there is no one like you lord, no one can touch my heart like you do, it is you lord why I have breath in my body, you are a shield and a strong tower from the enemy, you are my keeper, my very help in time of trouble, forgive me lord for my transgression and my sins only you have I sin against and done wickedly in your sight wash and cleans me lord, from my sins lead me in the path of righteousness for your name sake, let your will be done in my life in Jesus mighty name amen.

Daily Prayer

Father who art in heaven have mercy on me lord according to your loving kindness and your tender mercy thank you lord for a new day, thank you for saving grace let your will be done in me in Jesus' name. I repent lord from all my sins and my transgression renew a right spirit in me lord, close ever door lord that will bring destruction in my life, father dismantle every plot and plan of the enemy that comes to stop and block the purposes and plan that you have for me father replace my fear with faith and anxiousness with patience in Jesus' name. make a way where there seem to be no way in Jesus mighty name, and I will give you the honor and all the praise in Jesus' name amen.

Daily Prayer

Heavenly father you are awesome in this place mighty God. you are worthy to be praise there is none like you lord, no one can touch my heart like you do. you are alpha and omega the beginning and the end you are my strength. My hiding place in time of trouble thank you that I can find refuge in you the hope in whom I have believe. where can I go from your presence lord it is in you that I move and have my being. where can I run, I run to the rock of my salvation which is in you lord. Take me higher lord stretch me wider and father give me more grace to run this race because your word says it's not for the swift but for those that can endure to the end. so father give me the strength to run this race in Jesus mighty name and I will not rob you of your praise in Jesus mighty amen.

Daily Prayer

Heavenly father I call upon you to have mercy on me lord, forgive me lord of all my sins and my transgression. Father you are good, and your mercy is forever you have been good to me lord and I want to say thank you. Thank you, lord, from the bottom of my heart and the depts of my soul.

I come surrendering my life to you lord. Withholding nothing I give you my heart. my mind. my will in Jesus' name, I surrender every area of my life. lord let your will be done in me and through me in Jesus name Father let the plans you have for me be plain to me, so I do not walk-in error, father make every crooked path in my life straight. Every mountain be brought low in Jesus name. thank you for being my shepherd and the lifter up of my head in Jesus name amen.

Daily Prayer

Our father who art in heaven I come before you this day lord in reverence in worship to you lord. you are mighty in battle thank you lord for your redeeming blood thank you for the angels you have set to watch over me so that my foot will not dash against a stone. father forgive me of all my sin and my transgression bolt out my iniquity and my sin that is so ever before you in Jesus' name. lord whatever you do in this season don't do it without me, lord remember me o lord I am standing in need of prayer do not turn you face from me because of my sin, have mercy on me lord according to your loving kindness and your tender mercy come to my aid o lord, you are a mercy god keep me from self-destruction and restore unto me the joy of my salvation in Jesus mighty name.

Daily Prayer

Father who art in heaven I call upon you lord forgive me lord for every sin I commit that I am not aware of, out of ignorance. But known to you, I ask you for mercy lord you said in Exodus 34:6-7 that you are a compassionate and gracious god, slow to anger, abounding in love and faithfulness, maintaining love to thousands, and forgiving wickedness, rebellion, and sin. Yet you do not leave the guilt unpunished; you punish the children and their children for the sin of the parent to the third and fourth generation. So, lord forgive me that my sin will not be a HINDERANCE to my children and my children's children in JESUS mighty name I stand in the gap for the next generation to come in Jesus MIGHTY name may they walk with power an authority and clarity in the path they should take in Jesus might amen.

Daily Prayer

Father who art in heaven come into my heart, purge me with hyssop and I shall be white as snow cleans me in you blood, father forgive me of all my sins as I present my body to you as a living sacrifice, let your will be done in me and through me in Jesus name lord teach me your ways create in me a clean heart and renew a right spirit with in me. lord teach me how to conform to your will so I may not mis my season or what you would have me to do. Thank you, lord, for all that you have done for me and what you are about to do in Jesus mighty name amen.

Daily Prayer

Heavenly father have mercy on me lord according to your loving kindness and your tender mercy forgive me lord of all my sinful ways wash me with your blood thank you for another day that I can come before you in Jesus' name, I bring my thought into captivity in Christ Jesus. I pull down every strong hold that come to torment, confuse and mis lead me to act in an ungodly way. Your word says in Psalms 37[NIV] that we are to commit our way to you lord and trust in you so father I am committing my ways to you and my total dependency is on you make every crocked path straight in my life in Jesus' name amen.

Nightly Prayer

Heavenly father I thank you for keeping me throughout this day, thank you lord for your blessing that you have bestowed on me today. lord as I lay my head to sleep, I commit my body, soul and spirit to you. keep me from the terror that fly by night. Father make every crooked path straight in my life in Jesus name. father you speak to us in dreams and visions, so lord make my dreams and vision be clear to me lord and give me rest from day to day in Jesus' name amen.

Nightly Prayers

Heavenly father thank you for keeping me throughout this day. Hear my prayer o lord fight against them that fight against me. Do not let my enemies over power me. your word said in Psalms 34 NIV] that those who look to you are radiant their face is never covered with shame your word says blessed is the one who takes refuge in you, rescue me o lord from my enemies. You word says your eyes are on the righteous, and your ears are attentive to their cry; so, hear my cry o lord if I have sin against you forgive me o lord as I present my body to you as a living sacrifice tonight as I lay to sleep, I give you my soul to keep in Jesus name amen.

Nightly Prayers

Emmanuel the God that is with me as I approach your throne of grace may you grant me mercy in Jesus' name. forgive me lord of all my sins only you have I sin against and done wrong in you sight lord help me with my weaknesses because they are too much for me lord, but you said to Paul in 2 Corinthians 12:9[KJV] that your grace is sufficient in our weakness and your power is made strong in weakness so lord grant unto me your strength. As I am face with temptation each day. Let your power rest upon me lord so I my delight in insult, in hardship, in persecution and in difficulties in Jesus name. I commit my spirit to you tonight lord make my dreams and vision be clear unto me. And father I love you lord, in Jesus name amen.

Nightly Prayer

Father in the name of Jesus I honor your name you are mighty, and you are merciful towards us, forgive me lord for all my sins and my transgressions. I just want to say thank you for another day that I can come before you. thank you holy spirit for leading me and directing me on today thank you lord that you never leave us comfortless and without no sense of direction thank you lord for your blessing on today as I lay down to sleep, I give you my soul to keep in Jesus' name mighty amen.

Nightly Prayers

Father in the name of Jesus I give you the honor and all the praise lord I thank you for being my defense and my shield day by day, this is the day that you have make and I will rejoice and be glad in it. I will not be afraid of the terror at night nor the arrow that flies by day, nor the pestilence that stalks in the darkness, all the other gods they are the works of men, but you are the most high god there is none compare to you lord my loving and compassionate father. Tonight, as I lay my head down to sleep, I give you my soul to keep in Jesus mighty name amen.

Each one of us has the ability to be creative as sons and daughters of Elohim it is on the inside of all of us because we were made in his image and in his likeness, but we need to tap into it when we become a born-again believer.

I set out to ask individual why they pray, and these are their individual responses.

I pray for, instruction and to receive what god has for me. I pray to have a deeper relationship with God. I pray to give the lord thanks for is faithfulness, grace, and mercies and to glorify him always.
P.B.R.

I pray because it's a communication between me and God. Prayer gives me strength and I am reminded in prayer that God is with me, and he gives me direction when I pray.
O.R.H.

It gives me access to his divine will for my life. In addition, prayer allows me to be in the presents of the king of kings. While developing a supernatural ability to have a dialogue with him.
E.D.A.

I pray to acknowledge his existence and relevance in my life. I pray to bring his influence from heaven to earth.
L.B.

I pray to thank to the lord; I pray for spiritual empowerment. And I pray to speak to the lord.
M.C.

I PRAY because I feel safe talking to God, I pray because I know GOD will listen and understand and I pray because I want to build a better relationship with God
S.C

I pray because it is my time to talk with God, I pray to God for direction and sometimes Though nervous correction. I pray because God says I should. He knows there are some answers that I can't get from anyone else.
A.M.

I PRAY because that's how I communicate with God. Prayer makes me feel as if I am talking to God face to face. Prayer builds my faith in God.
C.H.

I PRAY because it soothes my soul. I pray because it opens heaven to respond to my requests. I pray because it is a necessary part of my relationship with my God.
P.M.T.

WHY DO YOU PRAY; _____

_____

_____

_____

_____ (write on the blank line.

The Power Of Prayer

TESTIMONIES- A few years ago, I was traveling with two of my colleagues we went to minister at a church and people were being delivered, heal, and set free in the name of Jesus. on our way back home, I was in the back of the car and the spirit of the lord reveal to me that we should pray against accident, from where we were coming from to our destination was two and a half hours drive. I told my colleagues at the time that we need to pray so we started to pray as we were praying on one accord against accident, we could sense such a great presence in and around the car we knew then we had heavenly escort. I remember like it was yesterday there was this white van speed by us and I heard a loud bang the van collide with a truck and caught on fire my colleague that was driving pull over and try to help the driver to exit the vehicle as it was on fire, just a reminder we were still praying when this was happen we realize that what the enemy planed for us was being over turn, glory be to God, no one got kill the driver walk away with a couple of scratches thanks be to God, we knew it was meant for us but God divert the plan of the enemy, the power of a praying person is effective in Jesus name.

One of the things I learn from this is not only the power of prayer but when you have people close to you or around your circle, they need to know who you are, your calling and giftings and trust that when you see or say something its truth been reveal by the spirit of God unto you,[test every spirit] it will take some time for them to get use to you but they must come to a realization of who you are and you're giftings in God. Jesus asks his disciples who do man say that I am and then he asks them who do you say that I am, who do you say that he is, it is very important. You must know the people that are around you for real, not just personality wise but spiritually and its going to take you walking in the spirit to know a person's true identity in God and also spending some quality time with them and they have seen the manifestation of what you say come to pass and the power of God manifest through you.

A few years ago, the lord gave me a vision and told me to pray and anoint my daughter's feet before she goes to school, I should have gotten up at that time in the night and pray like I always do but that night I did not got up and anoint her feet and pray, I said to myself I would have done it when I got up in the morning. In the morning I totally forget to do it rushing to get out the house, on that very day about 3pm in the afternoon I got an emergency phone call. when you are a parent or guardian you dread emergency phone calls. the lady on the line identified herself and ask if I was the parent then she started to explain the reason for her call and that my daughter had an incident, my heart started to beat faster and faster I took off from where I was to get to where she was, when I got to the scene there were resistant for me to get to see her, I remember bolting pass the person and I saw my daughter crying profusely there were emergency vehicles there one the scene. When she saw me, she said mom my knee it hurts as I look down at her knee her bone was pushing out, one of her knees was dislocated. I calm her down and held her hand as we try to lift her up so she could go into the ambulance, I went in the ambulance with her I thank God it could have been worse. If I had prayed that morning and anoint her feet, I know the incident would not have happen. You may say why didn't God stop it from happening? am glad you ask. my prayer was God hands to stop It from happening, he showed me what to do to prevented it from happening he gave me an instruction. God has given us dominion in the earth to dismantle the plots, plans and device of the wicked one the adversary the devil and if we do not position ourselves in God to stand up against him, he will have the freedom to attack us and leave an effect on us. and if we position ourself and ignore the people around us, meaning not praying and covering the people that are around us or the things that concerns us he will attack them, my brothers and sisters when he has no grounds to attack you, he will go after your children, your properties, your business and Anyone that is in your household, we must make sure that our household is in order watch and pray and be obedient to God. are we complying to Gods ordinance's, his commands and his precepts are we living a holy and sanctified life before God let us not leave any open doors to give the enemy access to invade our lives and please dont be ignorant of the devil's tactics he is already been defeated thank God for Jesus! Prayer can change things in Jesus mighty name. when we pray heaven respond and there is an open heaven over us, and access being granted in Jesus' name.

There is power in prayer to overturn the enemy's plans and schemes against our lives, it ignites the fire in and around us and keep us connected to the source of life Jehovah. A lot of us go through things like this story of my daughter's situation, some cause by disobedient and sometimes we become so busy we have no time to stop and pray in that very moment that God instruct us to do so, we put it off for another time and it became detrimental to us and the people that are around us. if we are truthful to ourselves it happens to the best of us. prayers when instructed by the lord and we disobey or delayed can be dangerous Especially when God gives you an instruction on what to do. Some of his instructions may look like foolishness to man but he knows what is ahead of us and what is about to take place if we do not pray in that very moment. in that season of my life, I was doing the work of the lord trying to fulfill one of my assignments. You see the enemy will try to bring chaos around you to distract you from your purpose or your assignment. You may be asking this question in your mind did I regret not praying for my daughter that morning, and the answer is yes, I do regret not praying for her that morning, but this situation has taught me that when God reveal anything to me or gives me an instruction on what to do, I try my best to move to it in that very moment and do not delay it. at times I would be somewhere, and the spirit of God moves up on me in prayer of intercession I go with the flow of the holy spirit, to be honest I will hesitate at times depending on where I am then move. sometimes we may think that people may look at us and think we are insane or its too much, but we must allow God to use our instruments for is glory as we present our bodies unto him as a living sacrifice, we must die daily from pride, self, and self-reliance because the flesh does not, please God. Carnal minded believers are one of our biggest critics as we walk with the lord, don't worry about what they think or say about you when you know that God is leading you, be confident in who you are in him and stand firm to what you know to be truth, in John 14:6 NIV Jesus said I am the way and the truth and the life. our life is not our own we belong to Jehovah, and he is the way, and it is in him that we move and have our being and it's the best place to be in him and allow him to lead and direct us. I have been in situation where I had to pray my way through it. prayer changes things for sure, I know because I tried it for myself, and I know prayer works and it is not that I only tried it during very hard times, but I seek God's presence earnestly on a daily basic it keeps me Intune with the spirit of God, it strengthens my faith in God, and keep my mind on him. LET me encourage you, be strong in the lord and in the power of his might, be brave and courageous, lean not to your own understanding but in all your ways acknowledge him and he shall direct your path. Acknowledge him for his faithfulness towards us, acknowledge him for he is great and greatly to be praise, acknowledge him for his unconditional love towards us, acknowledge him for his grace and mercy, glory be to GOD!!, acknowledge him for protecting you and keeping his word concerning your life because his plans for you is of good intention to bring you to an expected end hallelujah! Because he is an intentional God. Glory be to God! Acknowledge him for being a friend that sticks closer than a brother, acknowledge him for being our abba father, acknowledge him for is corrections when we need to be corrected, glory be God thank you lord. and acknowledge who he is the great I AM the only true and living God he is mighty in battle oh lift up your heads and be he lifted up and the king of glory shall come in who is this king of glory the lord strong and mighty he is the king of glory Psalm 24 KJV. Hallelujah!! I can say this without a shadow of a doubt that Jesus is the best thing that ever happen to me, and I am sure you can testify of his goodness and his manifold bless towards you I can say if you stick by him, he will stick by you. SHOUT UNTO GOD WITH THE VOICE OF TRIUMPH, HALLILUAH!

PSALMS 118:1-6, NIV Give thanks to the lord, for he is good; his love endures forever. Let Israel say: "his love endures forever." Let the house of Aaron say: "his love endures forever." Let those who fear the lord say: "his love endures forever." When hard pressed, I cried to the lord; he brought me into a spacious place. The lord is with me; I will not be afraid.

PSALMS 117:1-2 NIV. Praise the Lord, all you nation; extol him, all you peoples. For great is his love towards us, and the faithfulness of the Lord endures forever. Praise the Lord.

When Haman plot against Mordecai and his people and the order was sent out to destroy, kill and annihilate all the Jews when Mordecai heard he tore his clothes put on sackcloth and ashes and went out into the city wailing. When the word got to Esther she was in great distress, the bible says Esther sent cloth for Mordecai and he did not accept it. Esther then found out why Mordecai was wailing in sackcloth and ashes and with Mordecai instruction Esther fast and pray and went into the king for her people, she put her life in danger for her people. God has a purpose for your life that is bigger than where you are and bigger than your dreams and aspirations. Proverbs 19:21(NIV) Many are the plans in a person's heart, but it is the Lord's purpose that prevails.

Prayer

I declare and decree by the power and the authority of God that every mountain in my life be brought low in Jesus' mighty name.

I declare that every giant that has be assigned by the adversary to block or stop my progress be cut down now in the mighty name of Jesus.

I command that my mind will be in alignment with the spirit of God in Jesus mighty name. and As I delight myself in the lord May the manifestation of Gods word illuminates the atmosphere around me, around my home, on my job, in my business, around my family and wherever I go in Jesus mighty name.

I declare and decree that every evil hand that has stretched toward me and my household to interrupt and destroy my life be cut down in the mighty name of Jesus.

PSALMS 61: 1-3 NIV, hear my cry, o God; listen to my prayer. From the ends of the earth I call to you, I call as my heart grows faint; lead me to the rock that is higher than l. For you have been my refuge, a strong tower against the foe.

PSALMS 119 (read it)

A LITTLE ENCORAGEMENT TO THE BELIEVERS OF CHRIST JESUS; Be soberminded. Watch and pray ALWAYS, and in everything you do put Jehovah first, though they may rise against you stand in God with the belt of truth buckled around your waist, not just the belt but the whole armor of God, STAY FOCUS AND don't be distracted by the devices of the evil one THE ADVERSARY and the people that ALLOWS THE ENEMY TO USE THEM [THEY GIVE THE ENEMY ACCESS TO USE THEM] Romans 6:13 NIV) Do not offer any part of yourself to sin as an instrument of wickedness, but rather offer yourself to God as those who have been brought from death to life; and offer every part of yourself to him as an instrument of righteousness. fiery trials will come, PERSICUTION WILL COME but STAND IN THE AUTHORITY AND THE LIBERTY THAT GOD HAS GIVEN onto YOU IN JESUS MIGHTY NAME AMEN.

Matthew 10: 16 NKJV] "Behold, I send you out as sheep in the midst of wolves. Therefore, be wise as serpents and harmless as doves.

Acknowledgement

I GIVE THANKS and PRAISE TO THE HEAD OF MY LIFE THE BISHOP OF MY SOUL, MY REDEEMER, THE KING OF KINGS AND THE LORD OF LORDS JEHOVAH WHO HAS GIVEN ME THE KNOWLEDGE, REVELATION, AND INSPIRATION TO WRITE THIS BOOK. I GIVE HIM ALL THE HONOR AND ADORATION. WITHOUT HIM I WOULD NOT BE ABLE TO DO THIS. AS I acknowledge HIM DAILY, HE OPENS THE PATH FOR ME TO GO AND INSTRUCT ME ON THE THINGS I should do, because My life is not my own, I belong to JEHOVAH. Psalm 24:1; AMP The earth is the Lord's, and the fullness of it, the world, and those who dwell in it. Thank you, lord.

TO MY SUPPORTIVE TERM AND MY REMNANT SISTERS "ONE LOVE" WHO HAVE PRAYED WITH ME AND STAYED IN THE FIRE WITH ME, AND ENCORAGE ME when I feel discourage BE BLESS ALWAYS. A Special thanks to my eldest sister TOTHLYN AND TO THE BELIEVERS IN CHRIST, THE FIGHT IS ALREADY FIXED WE HAVE THE VICTORY IN JESUS mighty NAME AMEN.